Artists in Their Time

Alberto Giacometti

Jackie Gaff

Franklin Watts
A Division of Scholastic Inc.
New York Toronto London Auckland Sydney
Mexico City New Delhi Hong Kong
Danbury, Connecticut

First published in 2002 by
Franklin Watts
96 Leonard Street
London EC2A 4XD

First American edition published
in 2002 by Franklin Watts
A Division of Scholastic Inc.
90 Sherman Turnpike
Danbury, CT 06816

Series Editor: Adrian Cole
Series Designer: Mo Choy
Art Director: Jonathan Hair
Picture Researcher: Diana Morris

A CIP catalog record for this title
is available from the Library of Congress.

ISBN 0-531-12224-7 (Lib. Bdg.)
ISBN 0-531-16617-1 (Pbk.)

Printed in Hong Kong, China

Acknowledgements

AKG London: 16b, 34t. Paul Almasy/Corbis: fr cover bc, 34c. James L. Amos/Corbis: 31t.Bettmann/Corbis: fr cover
br, 24b, 25, 38t. Stephan Bianchetti/Corbis: 13t. © Henri Cartier-Bresson/Magnum Photos: 6t, 22b, 26t, 30t.
Christie's Images: 12t. Corbis: 24t. Galerie Jeanne Bucher, Paris: 12b. Galerie Daniel Malingue, Paris:
Giraudon/Bridgeman fr cover bl & 10t. Alberto Giacometti Foundation, Kunsthaus Zurich: 8b © ADAGP, Paris &
DACS, London 2002, 23 © ADAGP, Paris & DACS, London 2002. Terence le Goubin/BIPS/Hulton Archive: 31b.
Günter Graefenhain/Britstock-IFA: 38b, 41b. Hulton Archive: 8t, 41t, 42. Hulton/Corbis: 22t. Kunsthaus Zurich:
Bridgeman 11 © ADAGP, Paris & DACS, London 2002. Lapi-Viollet: 26b, 30b. David Lees/Corbis: 32t. Lipnitski-
Viollet: 36b. Pierre Matisse Gallery Archives, The Pierpont Morgan Library, New York: 28b. Lee Miller Archive: 20t.
The Museum of Modern Art, New York. Purchase. Photograph © 2002 The Museum of Modern Art, New York 17 ©
ADAGP, Paris & DACS, London 2002. National Gallery of Art Washington. Ailsa Mellon Bruce Fund. Photo Philip
A. Charles 19 © ADAGP, Paris & DACS, London 2002. Öffentliche Kunstsammlung Basel: 16t © ADAGP, Paris &
DACS, London 2002. Gianni Dagli Orti Archives/Corbis: 28r. Photos12.com-Bertelsmann Lexikon Verlag: 18t.
Private Collection: Bridgeman fr cover c © ADAGP, Paris & DACS, London 2002; 14; 27 © ADAGP, Paris &
DACS, London 2002, 29 © ADAGP, Paris & DACS, London 2002, 33 © ADAGP, Paris & DACS, London 2002, 35
© ADAGP, Paris & DACS, London 2002. Private Collection: 21 © ADAGP, Paris & DACS, London 2002. Photo
RMN-Hervé Lewandowski: 32. Scottish National Gallery of Modern Art, Edinburgh: Bridgeman 15 © ADAGP, Paris
& DACS, London 2002. Schweizer Eidgenossenschaft: Artothek 9t © ADAGP, Paris & DACS, London 2002.
Schweizerische Stiftung für die Photographie: 6b © The Giacometti Family, 10b © Sabine Weiss, 14c © Jacques-
André Boiffard, Centre Georges Pompidou, Paris. Scrovegni (Arena) Chapel, Padua: Giraudon/Bridgeman 9b.
SMPK, Berlin: Erich Lessing/AKG London 18b. Jon Sparks/Corbis: 7b. Tate Gallery, London: 13b © Salvador Dali,
Gala-Salvador Dali Foundation, DACS, London 2002, 37 © ADAGP, Paris & DACS, London 2002, 40 © ARS, NY
and DACS, London 2002. Sabine Weiss/Rapho/Network: 39 © ADAGP, Paris & DACS, London 2002.

Whilst every attempt has been made to clear copyright
should there be any inadvertent omission please apply
in the first instance to the publisher regarding rectification.

Contents

Who Was Alberto Giacometti?

The Swiss sculptor and painter Alberto Giacometti was one of the most original and important artists of the 20th century. His work changed our way of looking at the world. Although he was best-known for the tall, skinny statues he sculpted during the late 1940s, Giacometti was first introduced to art through drawing. He continued to draw and paint, as well as sculpt, throughout his life.

▲ The Giacometti family home in Stampa, Switzerland.

▲ The Giacometti family in 1909. From left to right: Alberto, Diego (front), Bruno, Giovanni, Ottilia, and Annetta.

BORN IN THE MOUNTAINS

Alberto Giacometti was born just over 100 years ago, on October 10, 1901. He was the eldest child of Giovanni Giacometti and his wife Annetta Stampa-Giacometti.

When Giacometti was born, his parents were living in the small village of Borgonova, which is in the southeastern Swiss Alps, in the narrow valley of the Bregaglia. In 1904 they moved their young family to the nearby village of Stampa, which remained their home for the rest of their lives. In 1909, the family inherited a second home in Maloja, at the top of the pass leading out of the Bregaglia valley. They spent their summers there from 1910 onward.

TIMELINE ▶

October 4, 1900	October 10, 1901	1902	Autumn 1904	1906	1913	1914
Alberto's parents, Giovanni Giacometti and Annetta Stampa, are married.	Alberto Giacometti is born.	Giacometti's brother Diego is born.	The Giacometti family moves to Stampa. Ottilia is born.	Bruno, the youngest child, is born.	Giacometti makes his first oil painting, a still life with apples.	Giacometti creates his first sculpture, a bust of his brother Diego.

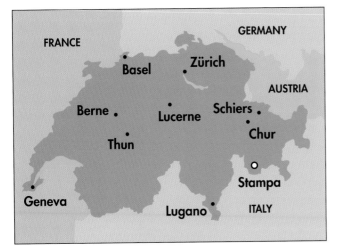

▲ Map of Switzerland. The town where Giacometti grew up, Stampa, is in the mountains close to the Italian border.

"There was no greater joy for me than to run to the studio as soon as school was out and sit in my corner near the window, drawing or looking at books."

Alberto Giacometti

AN ARTISTIC CHILDHOOD

Giacometti began drawing at an early age by creating illustrations for the books he read. The first drawing he remembered doing showed the fairytale scene of Snow White lying in her coffin, surrounded by the seven dwarves.

Giacometti's father, Giovani, and his godfather, Cuno Amiet, were artists. As a schoolboy, Giacometti was happiest when working in his father's studio. Giovanni encouraged Giacometti's developing skills as an artist, and his extensive library of art books provided an additional source of inspiration for his son.

From books, Giacometti learned about the great artists of the past, and studied and copied their work. A reproduction in an art book inspired him to make his first sculpture – a bust of his brother Diego, created in 1914 when Giacometti was 13 years old.

BREGAGLIA VALLEY

The village of Stampa is situated in the beautiful but harsh landscape of the Bregaglia valley, in southeastern Switzerland. The valley runs from the town of Castasegna in the west to Majola in the east. The River Mera, which cuts through the valley, flows south into Italy, fed by the cascading streams of the upper valley. The lower slopes, covered with fir trees and mountain pasture, lead up to the dominating jagged peaks and rocky cliffs that run the length of the valley.

▶ These steep slopes and jagged rocks are characteristic of the upper Bregaglia valley.

A Widening World

Giacometti's early education was at the village school in Stampa, but in 1915, a few months before his fourteenth birthday, he left home to go to boarding school in the village of Schiers. He loved it, and never seemed to have been homesick. His talent as an artist was obvious by this time, and Giacometti enjoyed the admiration of his teachers and fellow students – the school even allowed him to have a private studio.

◀ Geneva, c. 1900. Giacometti went to Geneva in the autumn of 1919 without finishing secondary school. However, he found that neither the School of Fine Arts nor the School of Arts and Crafts had anything new to teach him.

PAINTING OR SCULPTURE?

By the time he left secondary school in 1919, Giacometti knew he wanted to be an artist. However, at this stage, he didn't know whether he wanted to concentrate on painting or sculpture. In the end he studied both, attending the School of Fine Arts in Geneva, the capital of Switzerland, and then the nearby School of Arts and Crafts. Giacometti was lonely and unhappy in Geneva, and in May of 1920, he leaped at the opportunity to accompany his father on a trip to Italy.

A VISIT TO ITALY

In Italy, Giacometti was able to see great works of art with his own eyes, instead of in books.

Giacometti and his father mainly stayed in Venice, where the young artist was thrilled by the paintings of Tintoretto (1518-94).

◀ *Self-Portrait With Bird*, 1918, Alberto Giacometti.

TIMELINE ▶

August 1915	April 1919	May 1920	November 1920	December 1920	September 1921
Giacometti starts at boarding school, in the village of Schiers.	Giacometti moves to Geneva, to the School of Arts and Crafts.	Giacometti accompanies his father to Italy, visiting Venice and Padua.	Giacometti visits Florence, Italy.	Giacometti arrives in Rome, where he stays until mid-1921.	Giacometti witnesses death, prompting a lifelong fear of death.

Giacometti also visited Padua and saw the frescoes, or wall-paintings, of an even earlier artist, Giotto (c.1267-1337), which also had a great impact on him.

"It was like receiving a body-blow full on the breast."

Giacometti, on the effect of seeing Giotto's work

Giacometti adored Italy. After a short stay in Geneva, he returned there in November of 1920. He spent a few weeks in Florence then traveled to Rome, where he stayed with a relative's family for several months. There he fell in love with the eldest daughter, Bianca. Unfortunately she did not return Giacometti's affection and this upset him greatly.

▲ **Self-Portrait, c. 1923, Giovanni Giacometti.** Giacometti's father was also an artist, and studied in Paris at the Académie Julian. He took Giacometti to Venice because he had been asked to review works in the Biennale (see page 32).

▲ **The Lamentation of Christ, c.1305, Giotto.** This fresco is at the Scrovegni (Arena) Chapel in Padua, Italy. Giacometti was struck by the gentle expression and posture of Giotto's figures.

FEAR OF DEATH

In the autumn of 1921, Giacometti was invited to accompany an elderly Dutchman, Pieter van Meurs, on a trip to the Bavarian Alps. Tragically, within days, van Meurs fell ill and died. The 19-year-old Giacometti was alone at his bedside.

This traumatic experience awoke a fear of death in Giacometti that haunted him for the rest of his life. Simply being in the dark sparked terrors about dying, and he never slept without a light on again.

Early Years in Paris

By January of 1922, Giacometti had made up his mind to train as a sculptor. Taking his father's advice, he moved to Paris to study with one of the best-known sculptors of the time, Émile-Antoine Bourdelle.

Giacometti enrolled at Bourdelle's teaching studio at the Académie de la Grande-Chaumière. Over the next five years he studied at the studio, but also spent time away from the Académie, working on his own or visiting his family in Switzerland. In 1925, his brother Diego joined him in Paris and, two years later, the brothers moved into a tiny studio-apartment at 46 rue Hippolyte-Maindron. Giacometti continued to use this studio for the rest of his life.

▶ *Hercules the Archer*, 1909, Émile-Antoine Bourdelle.

DIFFERENT OPINIONS

Representational art attempts to portray people or objects in a way that captures their appearance in everyday life.

Abstract art, in contrast, uses non-representational shapes or colors, often to express the inner world of feelings and emotions. Although painters and sculptors had been experimenting with abstract art since the late 1900s, Giacometti's tutor, Bourdelle, firmly believed in the traditions of representational art.

Despite the differences in approach between teacher and student, it was Bourdelle's classes that laid the foundations for Giacometti's mastery of the art of sculpture.

ABSTRACT EXPERIMENTS

During his early years in Paris, Giacometti's work was representational – his sculptures depicted the actual shape of things in the real world. By the mid-1920s, he was beginning to experiment with abstract, or non-representational art – much to his tutor Bourdelle's disgust.

◀ This photograph, taken around 1927, shows the entrance to Giacometti's studio at 46 rue Hippolyte-Maindron in Paris. Initially Giacometti thought the space was very small but he gradually settled in, saying, "the longer I stayed there, the larger it grew."

TIMELINE ▶

January 9, 1922	February 1922	November 1925	April 1927	June 1929
Giacometti arrives in Paris to study with Antoine Bourdelle at the Académie de la Grande-Chaumière.	Giacometti's brother Diego joins him in Paris.	Giacometti shows his work for the first time, in the Salon des Tuileries, Paris.	The brothers move into a studio-apartment at 46 rue Hippolyte-Maindron, which they use for the rest of Giacometti's life.	Giacometti attracts the attention of the Surrealists.

Spoon Woman, 1926–27

bronze, 57 in (145 cm) high, Kunsthaus, Zürich, Switzerland

Giacometti's first major sculpture, *Spoon Woman*, was inspired by the human-shaped spoons used by the Dan tribe of Africa, which he had seen in a Paris museum. The largest and most dominant part of the sculpture is the bellylike bowl of the spoon. Above, the spoon handle seems to narrow into a waist, topped by breasts and a tiny, one-eyed head. Below the bowl, the legs have become the sculpture's pedestal, or base.

From Cubism to Surrealism

African tribal art, such as the Dan spoons that inspired Giacometti's *Spoon Woman* (page 11), played a key part in the development of new ideas about art. In 1907, the strangely distorted, unnaturalistic forms of African tribal masks had been a major inspiration for the revolutionary painting *Les Demoiselles d'Avignon* by Pablo Picasso (1881-1973). This painting and the work of Georges Braque (1882-1963) led to the development of the art movement which became known as Cubism.

> *"There was clearly a Surrealist atmosphere that influenced me."*
>
> *Alberto Giacometti*

African Dan spoon. The physical relationship between the Dan spoon and Giacometti's *Spoon Woman* (page 11) is clear. Giacometti simply adapted the round shape to suggest the figure of a woman.

Jeanne Bucher in her gallery. This was established in Paris in 1925 and was where Giacometti had his first major exhibition. Giacometti later exhibited much of his work at the Galerie Pierre – considered more important than the Galerie Jeanne-Bucher.

CUBISM

Cubism broke with traditional ideas of representation and gave Western artists the freedom to create abstract works of art. These works did not attempt to represent the world in a realistic way. Instead, artists depicted people, objects, and landscapes as geometric shapes, showing them from different angles at the same time.

Giacometti's early sculptures were greatly influenced by Cubism and the abstract work of contemporary sculptors such as Constantin Brancusi (1876-1957). He was also fascinated by the sculptures of prehistoric Greece and ancient Egypt.

In June of 1929, two of Giacometti's abstract sculptures were exhibited at the Galerie Jeanne-Bucher in Paris, and attracted the attention of the Surrealists.

SURREALISM

The Surrealist movement was founded in Paris in 1924 by the poet and critic André Breton (1896-1966). It drew on recent developments in psychology, or the science of the mind, and in particular, the research of the psychoanalyst Sigmund Freud (1856-1939) into the unconscious – the part of our mind we are not aware of.

Freud's studies had shown that the unconscious has an important role in shaping our thoughts, feelings, and actions. His work inspired the Surrealists to try to use their art to unlock their own unconscious in order to discover more about the hidden inner world of dreams, memories, and desires. The artist Max Ernst (1891-1976), for example, experimented with automatic drawing – letting images develop by chance, without conscious control. The Surrealists included some of

▲ A group of Surrealists: (from left to right) André Breton, Salvador Dali, Rene Crevel, and Paul Eluard (1895-1952). The Surrealists believed that Giacometti's sculptures showed the unconscious mind at work. Giacometti quickly became friends with Breton, whom he admired for his intelligence and self-confidence.

the most influential and creative people of the time, from the writer Louis Aragon to the artists Max Ernst, Joan Miró (1893-1983), and Salvador Dali (1904-89).

The Surrealists were so impressed with the work that Giacometti was doing that in 1931 Breton asked him to join the group.

◀ The Metamorphosis of Narcissus, 1937, Salvador Dali. The Surrealists were like a large family and both Dali and Giacometti were delighted to have Breton's approval for the work they were producing.

Surrealist Dreams

◀ *Lamp With a Bird* was designed by Giacometti for Jean-Michel Frank. A bird also appears in *Hands Holding the Void (Invisible Object)*, 1934 (page 19).

The inner world of our dreams embraces everything from peaceful fantasies to terrifying nightmares. Giacometti explored these dreams through Surrealism for only a few years in the early 1930s. During this time he produced some of his most disturbing works. Giacometti's Surrealist sculptures, like dreams, can be mysterious, beautiful, and frightening all at the same time.

Often, like the sculpture *Woman With Her Throat Cut* (right), they dealt with imagined death or violence. This piece looks as much like the twisted body of a spider as that of a woman. It seems to have evolved from an earlier sculpture, *Woman in the Form of a Spider*, which hung above Giacometti's bed for many years.

IN FASHION

In 1930, at about the same time as Giacometti was getting to know the Surrealists, he also became close friends with one of Paris's most successful and fashionable interior designers, Jean-Michel Frank. Giacometti began designing vases, candlesticks, lamps, and other decorative objects for Frank, working with the same dedication he applied to his art. "I realized that I was working on a vase exactly as I did on a sculpture," he said.

This wasn't his only venture into the world of fashion. For a while he also created jewelry for the Surrealist fashion designer Elsa Schiaparelli.

▲ A surreal view of Alberto Giacometti, 1931.

MOVING PARTS

During this time Giacometti made a number of sculptures that have moveable parts. *Woman With Her Throat Cut* has a cylindrical hand that can be moved into the leaflike hand on the right. This allows the viewer to interact with the piece.

TIMELINE ▶

1930	Spring 1931	June 1931	December 1931
Giacometti begins making decorative objects for the interior-designer Jean-Michel Frank.	Breton invites Giacometti to join the Surrealists.	Giacometti is extremely ill with appendicitis.	Giacometti's first published writings, *Objets mobiles et muets* (Moving and mute objects), appear in a Surrealist journal.

Woman With Her Throat Cut, 1932

bronze, 8 2/3 x 34 2/5 x 20 7/8 in (22 x 87.5 x 53 cm), Scottish National Gallery of Modern Art, Edinburgh, Scotland

Sculptures are often positioned on a base called a pedestal, but Giacometti wanted *Woman With Her Throat Cut* to be shown without one – it lies directly on the floor, making the viewer look down on it. Seen from far away, the sculpture looks like a half-squashed, giant insect.

"It was no longer the exterior forms that interested me but what I really felt."

Alberto Giacometti

Memories and Desires

Some of the Surrealists held Communist views and believed they should bring revolution not only to art, but also to society. Although he never joined a political party, in 1932 Giacometti became more closely linked with the political ideas of the Surrealists. He contributed to the "revolution" by drawing political caricatures and cartoons for their journals such as *La Lutte,* or "The Struggle."

Giacometti earned his living by selling his art to influential members of society so, to hide his identity, he signed his caricatures with the pseudonym Ferrache, or "Iron rod."

◀ *Atelier,* **1932.** Giacometti made this pencil sketch of his studio after constructing *The Palace at 4 A.M.* During the construction, he is said to have spent an entire six months in the studio without seeing the sun.

From time to time Giacometti described the personal meaning of a work. He did this for one of the most magical of his Surrealist sculptures, *The Palace at 4* A.M. (right). He linked it to a period when he spent many nights with a woman friend (Giacometti didn't give her name) building a fragile palace of matchsticks – but the palace kept collapsing and they had to start again. Although it's possible they really did build a matchstick palace, the image may also symbolize the fragility of their relationship.

▲ In the 1930s Communist leaders such as Joseph Stalin (above) attracted the support of many of the Surrealists.

INTERPRETATION

According to Giacometti, the wavelike shape toward the bottom right of the sculpture is a spinal column. This along with the pterodactyl-like bird are memories associated with his woman friend. The figure on the left-hand side is his mother. He identified himself with the central, oval-shaped object with a ball on it.

The sculpture doesn't reflect the reality of the everyday world, but instead the strangeness of memories and dreams.

TIMELINE ▶

1932	May 1932	May 1933
Giacometti moves closer to the Communist left of the Surrealists, and for awhile draws political caricatures for journals such as *La Lutte* "The Struggle."	Giacometti's first one-man art show is held at the Galerie Pierre Colle in Paris.	Giacometti publishes an account of his early life, *Yesterday, Quicksand,* in a Surrealist journal.

The Palace at 4 A.M., 1932-33

wood, wire, glass, and string, 25 x 28 1/4 x 15 3/4 in (63.5 x 71.8 x 40 cm), The Museum of Modern Art, New York, New York

The Palace at 4 A.M. was one of a number of Surrealist sculptures in which Giacometti experimented with a cagelike structure. In this case, the cage looks like a model for a stage set. Giacometti said that the figure on the left is his mother: "just as she appears in my earliest memories. The mystery of her long black dress touching the floor troubled me; it seemed to me like a part of her body, and aroused in me a feeling of fear and confusion." The three panels behind her are a curtain, "the very curtain I saw when I opened my eyes for the first time."

"We used to construct a fantastic palace at night… a very fragile palace of matchsticks."

Alberto Giacometti

Times of Change

▲ Giacometti in his studio. Many of his plaster and clay sculptures were destroyed before they could be cast in metal.

In June of 1933, Giacometti's father, Giovanni, died suddenly at the age of sixty-five. Giacometti rushed home to be with his family, but fell ill. It took several weeks' rest at the family's summer house in Maloja before he was ready to return to Paris. His interest in Surrealism and pure abstraction was fading, and for the rest of the year he produced very little new work.

TOWARD REPRESENTATION

Giacometti was starting out on the long search for a fresh way to express himself through his art. He wanted to create more representational images. In the spring of 1934 he began work on the mysterious *Hands Holding the Void* (right). In the summer of that same year he attempted his final abstract Surrealist sculpture – a tall cone with the puzzling equation "1 + 1 = 3" scratched into its base.

MAKING SCULPTURE

Giacometti usually began his sculptures in plaster or clay, building larger works up in stages around a metal framework called an armature. Bandages were wound around the armature and then covered in plaster or clay, which Giacometti would model with his fingers or carve with tools.

Afterward, if Giacometti was happy with it, the finished model would be copied in wood or stone, or cast in a metal such as bronze. Giacometti, however, was rarely satisfied with his work. He is famous for having destroyed many more pieces of sculpture than he ever kept.

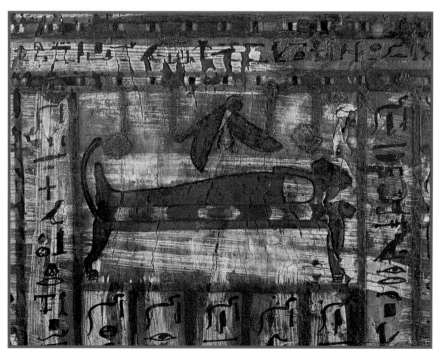

▲ Detail from the Ancient Egyptian sarcophagus of the priest Pai-es-Tenef. The "ba" (see right) is shown in the center of the picture, above the sarcophagus.

TIMELINE ▶

June 25, 1933	July 1933	Summer 1934
Death of Giacometti's father, Giovanni. Giacometti rushes home to Switzerland.	Giacometti falls ill and remains in Maloja for several weeks.	Giacometti designs the tombstone for his father's grave, and the carving is carried out by his brother Diego.

Hands Holding the Void (Invisible Object), 1934

bronze, 60 $\frac{1}{4}$ x 12 $\frac{3}{5}$ x 11 $\frac{4}{9}$ in (153 x 32 x 29 cm),
National Gallery of Art, Washington, D.C.

This is one of Giacometti's most puzzling sculptures – how can you grasp empty space? The stylized figure of the seated woman reflects the influence of the Ancient Egyptian sculptures that Giacometti admired (see left). This gives a clue to one possible interpretation. The Ancient Egyptians believed that a person's "ba," their memory and personality, lived on after death. They often depicted the "ba" or as a bird with a human head and arms. Giacometti has carved the right arm of the woman's chair into a bird shape – is he indicating that she is holding an invisible soul?

"I could have destroyed it.
But I made this statue for just
the opposite reason –
to renew myself."

Alberto Giacometti

Leaving the Surrealists

▲ Julien and Joella Levy outside the Julien Levy Gallery, New York, in 1932. Giacometti's exhibition here was not a success.

IN AMERICA

Giacometti's first U.S. exhibition was held in 1934 at the Julien Levy Gallery in New York. Giacometti had chosen the pieces himself, but the exhibition was not a success. The U.S. was still struggling with the effects of the Great Depression; millions of people were out of work, poor, and hungry.

It was not the best time to introduce what could appear as a frivolous new art form. The critic from *The New York Times* wrote: "Mr. Giacometti's objects, as sculpture, strike me as being unqualifiedly silly."

Throughout the time he was involved with Surrealism, Giacometti had been working mainly from memory and imagination. This was in harmony with the Surrealist focus on the inner world, as opposed to the outward reality of everyday life. However, by the autumn of 1934, Giacometti felt that he wanted to work directly from the natural world again and began to use real people as models.

To the Surrealist leader André Breton, this seemed like a betrayal. In December of 1934, Giacometti left the group before Breton could throw him out.

NEW MODELS

Giacometti's new models included his brother Diego and a woman called Rita. He attempted to sculpt their heads but, not satisfied with the results, destroyed almost all of his efforts. During this period, Giacometti wasn't only sculpting; he was also drawing and painting. Here he made slightly more progress, and kept some of his work including *The Artist's Mother* (right), which he painted during a visit to the family home in Switzerland.

◄ Giacometti's brother Diego, 1934. Giacometti made a number of sculptures of Diego, working with him in the morning. In the afternoon he worked with Rita and an English friend, called Isabel. Giacometti said, "I worked with a model all day from 1935 to 1940."

TIMELINE ▶

December 1934	December 1934	1936
Giacometti's first exhibition in the U.S. opens at the Julien Levy Gallery in New York. It includes his piece *Hands Holding the Void*. His work is received badly by the critics.	Giacometti officially leaves the Surrealists.	New York's Museum of Modern Art buys two of Giacometti's Surrealist sculptures.

The Artist's Mother, 1937

oil on canvas, 25 3/5 x 19 11/16 in (65 x 50 cm), Private Collection

In this portrait, the form of Giacometti's mother, Annetta, is built up from energetic light and dark lines. Giacometti was to develop this technique over the years, making it into a distinctly personal style – as you can see on page 37 in the portrait *Caroline*.

"I knew that…I would be obliged some day to sit down on a stool in front of a model and try to copy what I saw."

Alberto Giacometti

Smaller and Smaller

A busy Parisian street in the 1930s. Looking at street scenes like this inspired Giacometti to find other ways of representing the human figure.

TINY PEOPLE

Giacometti left a vivid description of what happened when he began to work from memory again:

"Wanting to create from memory what I had seen, I discovered to my terror that the sculptures became smaller and smaller. They had a likeness only when they were small, yet their dimensions revolted me, and tirelessly I began again, only to end up several months later at the same point again."

"A large figure seemed to me false and a small one equally unbearable. Then often they became so tiny that with one touch of my knife they disappeared into dust. Heads and figures seemed to me to have a bit of truth only when they were small."

The challenge for Giacometti was to find a way of making representational sculptures and paintings that didn't depict the outward, photographic reality of his model.

By 1937, his attempt to sculpt heads was going so badly that he decided to try whole figures again. He worked from memory instead of live models, but still focused on representation. He wanted to express a more individual view of his subject – what he felt about them, and his sense of their otherness, their separateness from himself. He had seen a friend in the distance one evening, and was intrigued by the fact that you can recognize people you know even from far away.

PIN-SIZED FIGURES

To his horror, something strange began to happen – his sculptures got much smaller. Figures ended up pin-sized, with pea-sized heads (see panel on left). It was a problem that troubled Giacometti for the next nine years.

Giacometti's sculptures really were very small. Some of them measured only a few inches.

TIMELINE ▶

1937	1938	Spring 1939	September 1939	June 1940	1941	1942
Giacometti paints, but struggles with his sculpture, which starts to shrink.	A traffic accident leaves Giacometti disabled.	Giacometti meets the philosophers Jean-Paul Sartre and Simone de Beauvoir.	World War II begins. Giacometti is turned down for Swiss military service because of his injured leg.	Giacometti flees Paris before the German army invades but returns shortly after.	Giacometti leaves Paris to visit his mother in Switzerland.	Giacometti travels to Geneva and stays there until 1945.

Small Figure on a Pedestal, 1940–45

bronze, 4 $\frac{2}{5}$ x 2 $\frac{4}{11}$ x 2 $\frac{1}{4}$ in (11.2 x 6 x 5.8 cm), Kunsthaus, Zürich, Switzerland

It may look fairly normal here, but the sculpture on top of this over-sized pedestal is less than an inch high. Creating a sense of the size of a person, and their distance away from you, is very difficult in sculpture – unlike in painting, where the artist can place figures against a background and show their size in comparison to other objects, such as a tree.

Conveying scale and distance became Giacometti's main concern when he began to sculpt whole figures from memory. One solution he found was to create a sense of scale by placing his tiny sculptures on pedestals that were large by comparison.

"To my terror the sculptures became smaller and smaller."

Alberto Giacometti

23

The World at War

While Giacometti struggled to cope with his shrinking sculptures, the world was drawing ever closer to war. In the summer of 1937, Pablo Picasso created his masterpiece *Guernica*, which condemned the German and Italian aerial bombing of the Basque town of Guernica during the Spanish Civil War (1936-39).

NEW FRIENDS

Around this time Picasso and Giacometti became friends. They spent hours together discussing their work. Other new friends included the Irish-born playwright Samuel Beckett (1906-89) who arrived in Paris in 1937, and the French Existentialist philosophers Jean-Paul Sartre (1905-80) and Simone de Beauvoir (1908-86).

▲ Guernica suffered great losses during the Spanish Civil War. Over 2,000 people were either injured or killed. The town was later rebuilt.

FOOT INJURY

In October of 1938, a few days after his thirty-seventh birthday, Giacometti was involved in a traffic accident that scarred him for life and would stop him from taking an active part in the approaching war.

Giacometti was walking home late in the evening when a speeding car swerved onto the pavement and knocked him down. Only his right foot was broken, but because he didn't follow the advice of his doctor, he was left with a limp for the rest of his life.

◀ The French philosopher Jean-Paul Sartre being interviewed by journalists. Sartre was very influential in the years during and after World War II. He believed in Existentialism, which is a way of thinking that says actions (the things you actually did) are more important than either beliefs or thoughts.

◀ French civilians flee before the advancing Germans arrive, 1940. Many artists in France fled to Britain and the U.S. during the war.

WAR!

Giacometti was staying at his family's summer home in Maloja when the Germans invaded Poland on September 1, 1939. He reported for Swiss military service the following day, but was declared unfit because of his foot injury. Although the situation wasn't clear at the time, Giacometti wouldn't have had to fight in any case: his homeland, Switzerland, remained neutral throughout the war. In mid-November, Giacometti returned to Paris with his brother Diego.

On June 5, 1940, Germany launched a major assault against France. As Swiss citizens, Diego and Giacometti probably had nothing to fear from the invaders. However on June 13, the day before German troops swept into Paris, the brothers, together with Diego's partner, Nelly,

attempted to escape to the south by bicycle. On June 14, the three of them came close to death when they were caught in the German bombing of the city of Etampes. Three days later they reached Moulins. Here they were overtaken by advancing German troops

and decided to return to Paris. They arrived back in Paris on June 22, the day the French government signed an armistice, or truce, with Germany.

TO GENEVA

In Paris, Giacometti's life remained normal for awhile. Then, in December of 1941, he applied for a visa to visit his mother in Switzerland. After a short stay, Giacometti moved to the Swiss capital, Geneva, where he stayed for the rest of the war, while Diego remained in Paris.

◀ German troops march into Paris, June 1940. The German occupation of Paris lasted until August of 1944 when they surrendered to the advancing Allied forces.

A New Direction

When Giacometti returned to Paris in September of 1945, he brought with him six matchboxes. Inside were all of the tiny sculptures he had kept from his years in Geneva. However, a breakthrough was on the horizon.

INSPIRATION

In February of 1946, Giacometti was watching a black and white movie newsreel. "Suddenly I no longer knew what it was I saw on the screen," he said. "Instead of figures moving in three-dimensional space, I saw only black and white specks shifting on a flat surface. They had lost all meaning." When, by contrast, he looked at the real people and objects around him, he saw them with fresh eyes – everything seemed "entirely new, fascinating, transformed, wondrous."

Giacometti returned to sculpting with fresh inspiration and enthusiasm. He began to make larger figures. To his surprise, Giacometti found that he could keep his sculptures taller by making them extremely thin.

▲ Giacometti and Annette in their favorite café in Paris, c.1960.

THE ARTIST IN LOVE

In 1946, Giacometti's Swiss girlfriend, Annette Arm, came to live with him in Paris. Three years later, on July 19, 1949, they married – to the great surprise of Giacometti's friends, who had all thought he would remain single forever.

Born on October 28, 1923, Annette was the daughter of a schoolteacher. She was just twenty when she met Giacometti in the autumn of 1943, having been introduced by a mutual friend in a Geneva café.

Annette became another important model for Giacometti's sculpture and paintings.

▲ The flat images seen on film inspired Giacometti to produce larger sculptures.

TIMELINE ▶

October 1943	September 1945	February 1946	July 1946	1947
Giacometti meets Annette Arm.	Giacometti arrives back in Paris.	While watching a movie newsreel, Giacometti has a visionary experience which is to transform his sculpture.	Annette Arm arrives in Paris, to live with Giacometti.	Giacometti makes the first of the tall, skinny sculptures for which he is now most famous.

Man Pointing, 1947

bronze, 70 2/5 in (179 cm) high, Private
Collection

Unlike the tiny figures Giacometti had
been making since 1937, this sculpture of
a man pointing is almost life-sized (nearly
6 feet high). Giacometti said that he
completed the final version during the
course of a single night, between
midnight and nine o'clock the following
morning. When the men from the metal
foundry arrived to take it away for
casting, the plaster was still wet. The
sculpture is one of the earliest of the tall,
skinny figures for which Giacometti is
now most famous.

*"I swore to myself that I
would no longer allow
my statues to shrink
even an inch."*

Alberto Giacometti

27

The Search for Truth

The years that Giacometti had spent wrestling with his tiny sculptures had been difficult. He had completed little work, and sold even less. Times were hard, and he had mainly survived on money borrowed from friends.

The New York based art dealer Pierre Matisse, son of the famous artist Henri Matisse (1869-1954), offered to exhibit and sell Giacometti's tall figures at his New York gallery. The exhibition opened in January of 1948 and was a huge success.

Giacometti had finally broken free from making miniature sculptures that had obsessed him for so long, and found a new style of sculpting. As a result, the late 1940s were very productive years for him, and he created many sculptures: of men and women on their own, and also in groups such as *City Square* (opposite).

STYLIZED BUT TRUE

These tall, skinny statues, with their rough surfaces, are stylized, and not at all naturalistic. Giacometti once wrote that, "the truer a work is the more stylized it is." For Giacometti, stylized work such as his own, or that of the prehistoric Greeks for example, came closest to expressing what he wanted to say through his art.

Although these tall, skinny sculptures are the works for which Giacometti is now most famous, most of them were produced during a three years period between 1947 and 1950.

▲ Cycladic figure, c.2500 B.C. Most of these prehistoric Greek figures were very different from any other sculpture of their time. With highly stylized features, including folded arms and flat, two-dimensional bodies, the figures look strangely modern.

Alberto Giacometti

▲ The front page of the catalog from Giacometti's 1948 exhibition at Pierre Matisse's gallery in New York.

TIMELINE ▶

January 19, 1948	July 19, 1949
A solo exhibition of Giacometti's new work opens at the Pierre Matisse Gallery in New York. It is a great success and establishes his reputation in the U.S.	Giacometti and Annette marry in a Paris registry office.

City Square, 1948

bronze, 23 x 17 $^1/_2$ x 9 $^6/_7$ in (58.5 x 44.5 x 25 cm), Private Collection

The walking figures in this sculpture are men, while the standing figure with its arms pressed closely to its sides is a woman. This contrast appears in nearly all of Giacometti's postwar sculptures – male figures are active, walking or pointing, while female figures stand still, frozen to the ground. The only walking woman appears in a sculpture called *Figure in a Box Between Two Boxes Which are Houses*, but she is trapped within a glass and metal case.

"The heads that come closest to resembling people I see on the street are those that are the least naturalistic."

Alberto Giacometti

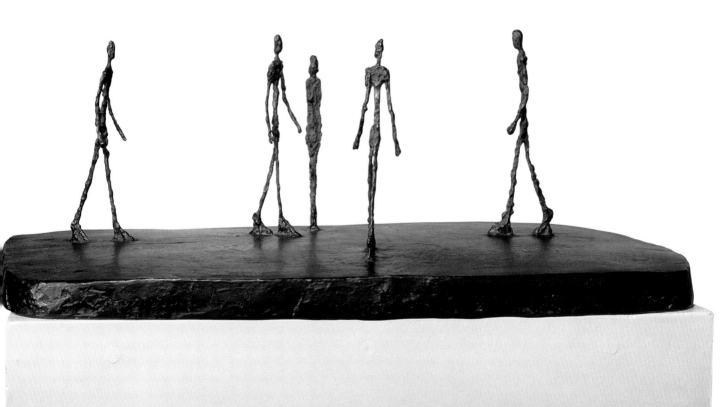

Interpretations

While Giacometti concentrated on his sculptures, other people were busy trying to make sense of his work.

FRAGILE EXISTENCE

Giacometti's friend, the Existentialist philosopher Jean-Paul Sartre (see page 24), had many ideas that rejected traditional beliefs. Sartre believed that human existence was meaningless and fragile, liable at any time to end abruptly by death. He thought that this and other Existentialist ideas were being expressed by Giacometti's tall sculptures – with their fragile thinness, which makes them look as if they are about to fade away to nothing.

Sartre outlined his thoughts about the meaning of Giacometti's work in the catalog for Giacometti's 1948 exhibition at the Pierre Matisse Gallery in New York. Many others also began to link Giacometti's work with the Existentialist way of thinking.

▲ Giacometti photographed on a wet day in Paris, 1961. Although, like many artists, he often worked alone in his studio for hours at a time, Giacometti argued that he never intended his work to be about loneliness.

MODERN CITY LIFE

For others, even today, Giacometti's sculptures speak simply of the loneliness of modern city life: the crowds that flow along during rush-hour, never meeting each other's eyes or stopping to exchange a friendly word; the many people who live alone and friendless, surrounded by millions of other faceless city-dwellers.

◄ A Paris back street, c.1950. Most cities can be lonely places to live.

PATTERNS MADE BY PEOPLE

Giacometti always said that he never intended his work to express Existentialism or loneliness. "In the street the people astound and interest me," he said. He then went on to describe watching a scene that seems very similar to his sculpture *City Square* (see page 29): "Every second the people stream together and go apart… The men walk past each other, they pass without looking. Or else they stalk a woman. A woman is standing there and four men direct their steps more or less towards the spot where the woman is standing." For Giacometti, it wasn't loneliness that he saw around him, but the living patterns made by people as they interacted with each other.

▲ A typical city street at night, 1950s. Many people believe Giacometti's sculptures represent the feelings of fear and desire which are a feature of modern city life.

DIFFERENT VIEWPOINTS

This does not mean it is wrong to find other meanings in Giacometti's work. Each person who views a work of art is allowed their own personal understanding of what it means to them. Great works of art can have no single interpretation for the viewer. They mean different things to different people, at different times in their lives.

"It's the totality of this life that I want to reproduce in everything I do."

Alberto Giacometti

◄ One of the best ways to interpret art such as Giacometti's is to discuss it in a group.

Growing Fame

▲ Giacometti's tall, skinny sculptures on display at the Venice Biennale in Italy, 1956.

uring the late 1940s Giacometti worked with intense energy on his tall, skinny sculptures. Often, he had the entire piece figured out in his mind long before he began working on it. This was the case with *The Chariot* (right):

"In 1947 I saw the sculpture before me as if it were finished," Giacometti said, "and in 1950 it became impossible for me not to make it." He explained that one of the inspirations for the piece was the "tinkling" medical cart that was wheeled through the hospital where his foot was being treated, after he was run over by a car in 1938 (see page 24).

FAME AND FRIENDSHIP

Giacometti's work was becoming well-known in artistic circles, and his fame was spreading. In 1950, he was invited to take part in the Venice Biennale. This prestigious exhibition, the first held in 1895, has been a showcase for avant-garde art since the late 1940s, and is held every two years in Venice, Italy.

It was a great honor for Giacometti to be selected, but when he arrived in Venice and found that the sculptures of an old friend, Henri Laurens (1885-1954), were hidden in the background, Giacometti refused to take part and withdrew his sculptures. Loyalty to friends was more important to him than fame.

It wasn't until 1956 that Giacometti's sculptures were shown at the Biennale.

ART FOR A PUBLIC PLACE

Giacometti made *The Chariot* in response to a request from the local council to provide a statue for a public square in northern Paris. The authorities were shocked by the finished work and rejected it. Today, however, many people consider it as the most impressive of all the tall, skinny sculptures that Giacometti created during the postwar years.

► An ancient Etruscan incense burner in the form of a boy on a four-wheeled chariot, c. late 6th century B.C. Giacometti may have been influenced by art such as this in making *The Chariot* (opposite).

TIMELINE ►

Summer 1950	November 1950
Giacometti withdraws his work from the prestigious Venice Biennale out of loyalty to his friend, Henri Laurens.	A second exhibition at the Pierre Matisse Gallery, New York, is even more successful than the first.

The Chariot, 1950

bronze, 56 in (142.2 cm), Private Collection

Raised on its twin plinths, this sculpture cannot actually roll across the floor because its wheels are fixed and will not turn. As with Giacometti's other tall, skinny sculptures, the figure itself is anchored by its massive feet. Yet *The Chariot* suggests both stillness and movement. Unlike Giacometti's other female figures, this woman's arms are not pressed tightly to her sides. Instead, they are held away from her body, making her look poised for movement – as though the chariot's wheels might roll and sweep her onward to some mysterious destination.

"I saw the sculpture before me as if it were finished."

Alberto Giacometti

Fresh Insights

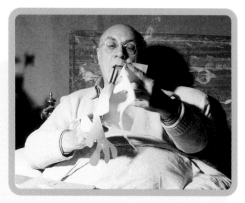

▲ French painter and sculptor Henri Matisse cutting out his paper shapes, 1948.

FRESH MODELS

Throughout his life, the chief models for Giacometti's sculptures, drawings, and paintings were his brother Diego, his mother Annetta, and his wife Annette.

During the 1950s, he also began to use friends as models, including the philosopher Jean-Paul Sartre, the composer Igor Stravinsky (1882-1971), and the writer Jean Genet (1910-86). Giacometti became friends with Genet in 1954 and was fascinated by his round, bald head.

Another famous model was the artist Henri Matisse, whom Giacometti sketched in the summer of 1954, before sculpting a medallion of Matisse for the French mint.

Throughout his life Giacometti continued to explore his art, and in the early 1950s he made another new start. Since 1947 he had been working mainly from memory, sculpting his skinny, full-length figures. Now, in drawing, painting, and sculpture, he began to use real people as models again and focused on half-figures (from the waist, chest, or shoulders up). The chest or shoulders of his subject formed the pedestal of the sculpture, while the head – particularly the eyes and their gaze – became increasingly important.

"One day when I was drawing a young girl," Giacometti explained, "I suddenly noticed that the only thing that was alive was her gaze. The rest of her head meant no more to me than the skull of a dead man… I began to see living beings exclusively through their eyes."

◄ A photograph of Giacometti at work. He is carefully shaping one of the half-figures that became his main focus during the 1950s.

"If the gaze is the main thing, then the head becomes the main thing."

Alberto Giacometti

TIMELINE ▶

c.1950	June 1951	November 1951	1954	Summer 1956
Giacometti makes another fresh start in his art.	A solo exhibition of Giacometti's postwar work opens at the Galerie Maeght in Paris, and establishes his reputation in Europe.	Giacometti and Picasso quarrel, bringing their friendship to an end.	Giacometti becomes close friends with the writer Jean Genet.	Giacometti's work is first shown at the Venice Biennale.

Bust of Diego, 1954
bronze, 14 1/4 in (36.3 cm) high, Private
Collection

When viewed from the front, the heads of
many of the busts Giacometti sculpted
during the 1950s are extremely thin,
echoing the slenderness of the earlier, full-
length figures. When it came to modeling
the eyes, Giacometti focused on the
curve of the eyeball. When that was
right, he said, the eye sockets,
nostrils, nose, and mouth
would follow – "and all of
this together might just
produce the gaze."
He often scratched
a vertical line in
place of the pupil.

*"Diego has posed ten
thousand times
for me."*

Alberto Giacometti

A New Model

WAITING FOR GODOT

Although during the early 1960s Caroline was Giacometti's main model, she was not the only one, and he was also carrying out other work. Early in 1961 an old friend, the writer Samuel Beckett, asked him to design the stage set for a new production of his play, *Waiting for Godot*.

Giacometti had never done anything for the theater before and was delighted to be asked. His set design was as stark as the play's plot, in which two vagrants wait for someone called Godot, who never arrives. The stage was entirely bare, except for Giacometti's sculpture of a single, plaster tree.

▲ Giacometti with "Caroline" and her dog Merlin, c.1963.

▲ Giacometti's stage set for *Waiting for Godot*. The thin tree emphasizes the emptiness of the stage.

During the 1950s, the relationship between Giacometti and Annette grew more stormy, however, Annette continued to pose for him. By the end of the decade, Giacometti was leading a separate life from his wife.

"CAROLINE"

In October of 1959, Giacometti met a young woman who went under the pseudonym of "Caroline" – she didn't want her real name to be known. Soon Giacometti was fascinated by her. Within a few months of their meeting, Caroline began posing for him and, for the next few years, she was his most frequent companion and model.

Giacometti made numerous drawings and paintings of Caroline, as well as sculpting a single bust. "She sits for me almost every evening from nine to midnight or one o'clock," he said in 1963. "In the past few years there haven't been more than four or five evenings that we haven't worked."

TIMELINE ▶

1958	October 1959	1961	1962	October 1962
Giacometti is commissioned to create sculptures for New York's new Chase Manhattan Plaza, although they are never installed.	Giacometti meets "Caroline," who is to be his chief model and companion for several years.	Giacometti designs the scenery for Samuel Beckett's play, *Waiting for Godot*.	Giacometti completes a series of eight busts of his wife, Annette.	Giacometti attends the opening of a major exhibition of his work in Zürich, Switzerland.

Caroline, 1965

oil on canvas, 51 2/11 x 35 in (130 x 89 cm), Private Collection

In Giacometti's paintings and drawings, the eyes and gaze of his model are just as important as they are in his sculptures. The structure is built up from strong black and white lines, at their most dense around the head, with sparing use of other colors.

"I try to paint with colors," Giacometti said, "but I can't apply colors without a structure to start with. To build up this structure on the canvas is already an endless undertaking. And to go on from there to color seems next to impossible."

The Final Years

▲ The New York skyline, 1964. It would have looked much the same a year later when Giacometti saw it from the deck of the *Queen Elizabeth*.

A FINAL VOYAGE

By the early 1960s Giacometti was one of the world's most famous living artists, and exhibitions of his work were being held nearly every year. His last overseas journey was in October of 1965, when he visited New York to attend an exhibition of his work at the Museum of Modern Art.

Giacometti refused to fly, and instead traveled with his wife Annette on the luxury liner, *Queen Elizabeth*. He couldn't swim though, and was as fearful of the ocean as he was of flying. Writing during the journey home, he said: "When I saw the distant point of New York dissolve... it was as though I were witnessing the beginning and end of the world."

Giacometti always worked in his studio until midnight or later. He would then break for a meal in a café followed by drinks, before returning to the studio to carry on until dawn. When he got up in the early afternoon, he was usually still exhausted from the night before.

HEALTH PROBLEMS

For years Giacometti had worked too hard, smoked too much, and slept and eaten too little. By the 1960s it was clear that his health was affected. He had suffered stomach aches for some time, but the pain became so bad that he went to see a specialist. In February of 1963, he was operated on for stomach cancer. Then, after a short rest, he returned to his usual way of life and all his old bad habits.

By late 1965, Giacometti was again feeling ill enough to see a doctor. The doctor advised Giacometti to go into the hospital for tests. He chose a hospital in the Swiss town of Chur, and traveled there by train on December 5. Tests showed that the problem wasn't cancer this time, but his heart. Caroline and his family gathered around him, and on January 11, 1966, Giacometti died. He was only sixty-five.

▲ The picturesque town of Chur in Switzerland where Giacometti died in 1966. The funeral was held in his birthplace, Borgonova, on January 15, 1966.

TIMELINE ▶

February 6, 1963	January 25, 1964	Summer 1965	December 6, 1965	January 11, 1966
Giacometti has an operation for stomach cancer.	Giacometti's mother, Annetta, dies.	Major exhibitions of Giacometti's work open in New York and London.	Giacometti checks into a Swiss hospital in Chur.	Alberto Giacometti dies in the hospital.

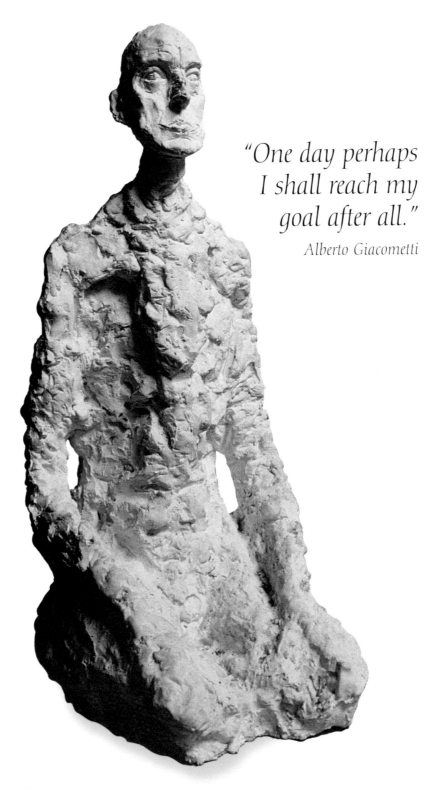

*"One day perhaps
I shall reach my
goal after all."*

Alberto Giacometti

Lotar III, 1965
bronze, 25 ¹/₂ x 9 ⁶/₇ x 13 ³/₄ in (65 x 25 x 35 cm), Private Collection, Switzerland

Among Giacometti's last works were three sculptures of the photographer Elie Lotar, who had been a friend since the late 1920s. Giacometti was still modeling this bust, *Lotar III,* during his last days in Paris before leaving to go into hospital in Chur.

    After his death, Giacometti's brother Diego had the sculpture cast in bronze and placed it on his brother's grave in Borgonova, the village where Giacometti was born, along with a small bronze bird that Diego had made himself.

Giacometti's Legacy

Giacometti was one of the most individual and committed artists of the 20th century, and his influence on both painting and sculpture has been immense. Once he had achieved his uniquely personal style, it was virtually impossible for any artist that came after him not to be influenced in some way, particularly if their work was representational.

▲ **Vertical Spin, 1986-87, Susan Rothenberg.** The brushstrokes capture the flowing movements of a dancer, but also recall the energetic lines of Giacometti's portraits (see pages 21 and 37).

SUSAN ROTHENBERG (b.1945)

The American artist Susan Rothenberg, often labeled as a New Image painter, first became known in the 1970s for a series of paintings of horses, whose simplified style invokes the cave-paintings of prehistoric times.

For a while in the early 1980s, she painted pared-down figures that, like Giacometti's sculptures, seemed to suggest the loneliness and frailty of human life. At this stage in her development, Rothenberg's energetic brushstrokes and minimal use of color also showed the influence of Giacometti.

"If you're going to deal with the human figure, you're likely to bump into him [Giacometti]."

Susan Rothenberg

ELIZABETH FRINK (1930-93)

The British sculptor Elizabeth Frink was another artist whose work briefly reflected Giacometti's influence.

Frink was very excited when she saw Giacometti's tall, skinny sculptures at the Musée d'Art Moderne in Paris in the early 1950s, and she appears to echo them in her 1965 sculpture called *Standard*, in which an eagle perches on a tall, slender perch with a huge, footlike base.

OTHER ADMIRERS

Among the many other artists who spoke of their admiration for Giacometti was the French-born sculptor Louise Bourgeois (b.1911), who particularly liked Giacometti's portraits: "The people I like most," she said, "are interested in portraiture, the symbolic and recognizable unique essence of a person."

▲ Elizabeth Frink in 1953 with her sculpture *Man Who Has Suffered*. It has the same rough quality as Giacometti's later work. Notice the bird resting on the figure's hand which Giacometti also used in a number of his works (see page 19).

Willem de Kooning (1904-97), an American artist, expressed his appreciation more strongly. He said he had been "knocked out" by seeing Giacometti's sculptures at the 1948 exhibition in New York: "it looked like the work of a civilization, not one man."

Perhaps the most descriptive assessment, though, came from another American artist, Barnet Newman (1905-70): "Giacometti made sculptures that looked as if they were made out of spit," he said, "new things with no form, no texture, but somehow filled; I take my hat off to him."

▲ The Kunsthaus Museum in Zürich, Switzerland, houses the largest collection of sculptures by Giacometti.

Two Artists

In the world of art, Giacometti's most famous contemporary was the Spanish-born Pablo Picasso (1881-1973), one of the most renowned artists of all time.

▲ Picasso in 1937. Giacometti quickly became friends with Picasso, but it didn't last.

"One day Pablo seemed particularly pleased with a sculpture he had completed… Giacometti studied it and said: 'Well, the head is good, but perhaps you shouldn't leave the rest of it like that. Is that really what you intend to do? It seems to me it's more important for the work to exemplify the principle that's behind it than to benefit from some lucky accident…'

I think Giacometti was the one with whom Pablo felt most inclined to discuss such matters… As Pablo pointed out, Giacometti was always asking himself fundamental questions to clarify the real point of what he was doing."

▲ Picasso's biographer Françoise Gilot writing about the relationship between the two men.

THE ARTISTS MEET

Picasso was 20 years older than Giacometti, and was already extremely successful and well-known by the time Giacometti arrived in Paris in 1922. The two men met in the late 1920s, when Giacometti was becoming involved with the Surrealists, but it took another ten years for their friendship to develop.

TIMELINE ▶

1901	1920	1925	1932	1934	1938
October 10, 1901 Alberto Giacometti is born in Switzerland.	**May 1920** Travels with father to Italy, visits Venice and Padua.	**1925** First show of his work, at the Salon des Tuileries, Paris.	**1932** Moves to the Communist left, draws political caricatures.	**December 1934** His first exhibition in the U.S. receives bad reviews. Officially leaves the Surrealists.	**October 1938** Traffic accident leaves him disabled.
1913 Does his first oil painting.	**Nov-Dec** Visits Florence, then Rome. Stays for six months.	**1927** Moves into studio apartment with his brother Diego.	**May 1932** First one-man art show.	**1936** Museum of Modern Art, New York buys two of his Surrealist sculptures.	**Spring 1939** Meets Jean-Paul Sartre and Simone de Beauvoir.
1914 Does his first sculpture.	**January 1922** Arrives in Paris to study at Académie de la Grande Chaumière. Later, is joined by his brother Diego.	**1929** Noticed by the Surrealists.	**June 1933** Death of his father. Giacometti returns to Switzerland. Becomes ill.		**September 1939** World War II begins. Turned down for military service.
1915 Goes to boarding school.		**1931** Invited to join the Surrealists. Nearly dies from appendicitis. First writings are published.	**Summer 1934** Designs his father's tombstone.	**1937** Giacometti paints, but struggles with sculpture, which starts to shrink.	**June 1940** Flees Paris but later returns.
1919 Attends School of Arts and Crafts, Geneva.					

Giacometti was never among the flatterers that accompanied Picasso. He did not offer empty praise, and wanted Picasso to know that not "everyone is on his knees before him." Perhaps this is why Picasso developed a deep respect for Giacometti's opinions.

VISITING THE STUDIO

By the summer of 1937, Giacometti was a frequent visitor to Picasso's studio in the rue des Grands-Augustins. Françoise Gilot, Picasso's partner at that time, described how whenever Giacometti came to the studio, the two men "would discuss in the minutest detail whatever sculpture Pablo might be working on at the moment."

"Giacometti speaks of Picasso, whom he saw yesterday evening and who showed him some drawings. It seems that Picasso is happy when Giacometti says of his drawings: 'Yes, one sees some progress.'"

▲ Entry for May 17, 1946, in the diary of the writer and philosopher Simone de Beauvoir (1908-86).

"He's concerned with a certain illusion of space that is far from my own approach but it's something no one ever thought of before in just that way. It's really a new spirit in sculpture."

▲ Picasso talking about Giacometti.

STORM CLOUDS GATHER

The friendship between Picasso and Giacometti was always stormy. Picasso was just as likely to make fun of Giacometti behind his back as to praise him to his face. Although once describing Giacometti's contribution to art as "a new spirit in sculpture," Picasso made fun of Giacometti's tendency to destroy more work than he created: "Giacometti wants us to regret the masterpieces that he will never make," he said.

Eventually, Giacometti had enough. "One day I had to admit to myself that he [Picasso] was stealing my confidence with his insinuations and malicious criticisms," Giacometti explained. "I put a distance between myself and him, and became my old self again. Picasso is someone who has the tendency to take his models apart, to destroy everything he touches." Sadly, by the early 1950s, the friendship came to an end.

1941	1947	1950	1959	1962	1965
1941 Visits his mother in Switzerland.	**1947** Makes the first tall, skinny sculptures.	**November 1950** Second successful exhibition at the Pierre Matisse Gallery.	**October 1959** Meets Caroline, who becomes his main model and companion.	**October 1962** Travels to Zürich, Switzerland, for opening of a major exhibition of his work.	**Summer 1965** Major exhibitions of Giacometti's work in New York and London.
1942 Travels to Geneva, stays there until 1945.	**1948** Solo exhibition at the Pierre Matisse Gallery in New York is a great success.	**Summer 1956** First showing of his work at the Venice Biennale.	**May 1961** Designs sets for Samuel Beckett's play *Waiting for Godot*.	**February 1963** Operation for stomach cancer.	**December 6, 1965** Giacometti checks into hospital in Chur, Switzerland.
October 1943 Meets Annette Arm.	**July 19, 1949** Marries Annette.	**1958** Commissioned to create sculptures for New York's new Chase Manhattan Plaza, although they are never installed.	**1962** Completes a series of eight busts of his wife, Annette.	**January 25, 1964** Giacometti's mother, Annetta, dies.	**January 11, 1966** Alberto Giacometti dies in hospital.
September 1945 Returns to Paris.	**Summer 1950** Withdraws work from Venice Biennale out of loyalty to his friend.				
1946 Annette Arm arrives in Paris, to live with Giacometti.					

Glossary

abstract: art that does not imitate the world around us. It is usually impossible to recognize objects, people, or places in abstract art.

armature: a structure, of wood or wire, hidden inside a model that helps to give it strength.

Biennale: a prestigious international art exhibition held in Venice every two years. The first one was in 1895.

bronze: a mixture of copper and tin that is often used to make metal sculptures.

bust: a sculpture showing a person's head and shoulders.

cast: in sculpture, to pour metal that has been heated until it is liquid into a pre-shaped mold. The metal then sets into the shape of the mold. Some sculptors also make early casts of their work using plaster so that they can shape it as they want before it is finally cast in metal.

Cubism: the name of an art movement based in Paris from about 1907, led by Pablo Picasso (1881-1973) and Georges Braque (1882-1963). The Cubists painted multiple viewpoints of people or objects so they could all be seen at the same time.

Existentialism: a philosophy popular in the 20th century which says that life has no meaning except for the actions that we take.

foundry: the place where metal is cast by being melted and then hardened in a mold.

Great Depression: the name given to the global economic slump of the 1930s.

interpretation: the meaning that someone sees in a work of art.

military service: when someone has to join the armed forces (for example, the army) for a set period of time.

naturalistic: describes art which tries to copy nature as closely as possible.

pedestal: what supports a column or statue (based on the Latin word *pedes* meaning "feet").

philosopher: someone who examines scientific principles and human beliefs.

plaster: a fine white powder which sets solid when mixed with water. Sculptors sometimes use it to make a plaster cast of their sculpture to get the shape right.

plinth: a square-shaped block on which a sculpture rests.

psychoanalysis: a form of mental healing pioneered by Sigmund Freud (1856-1939). It tries to alter the personality in a positive way by exploring and freeing the unconscious mind.

representational: describes art which is designed to depict a likeness of the world around us. It is the opposite of abstract.

sculpture: a three-dimensional work of art. Sculpture is sometimes carved out of wood or stone, and sometimes modeled first and then cast in metal.

studio: an artist's workshop.

stylized: describes art that represents people and objects in a very particular and distinctive, often non-realistic way.

Surrealism: an art movement that emerged in the 1920s that tried to depict the life of our unconscious minds, or dreams. Its most famous artist is Salvador Dali (1904-89).

unconscious: the deepest areas of the mind, where we have feelings, memories, and emotions of which we are not aware.

Museums and Galleries

Works by Giacometti are exhibited in museums and galleries all around the world. The ones listed here have work by Giacometti on permanent exhibition, but most also display a wide range of other artists' works, too.

Even if you can't visit any of these galleries yourself, you may be able to visit their web sites. Gallery web sites often show pictures of the artworks they have on display. Some of the web sites even offer virtual tours which allow you to wander around and look at different paintings while sitting comfortably in front of your computer.

Most of the international web sites detailed below include an option that allows you to view them in English.

Art Gallery of Ontario
317 Dundas Street West
Toronto, Ontario
M5T 1G4
Canada
www.ago.on.ca

Centre National d'Art et de Culture Georges Pompidou
75191 Paris
cedex 04
France
www.centrepompidou.fr

Hirshhorn Museum and Sculpture Garden Smithsonian Institution
Independence Avenue at 7th Street, SW
Washington, DC 20560-0350
www.hirshhorn.si.edu

Kunstmuseum, Basle
St. Alban-Graben 16
CH-4010 Basle
Germany
www.kunstmuseumbasel.ch

Kunsthaus, Zürich
Home place 1
8024 Zürich
Switzerland
www.kunsthaus.ch

Peggy Guggenheim Collection
Palazzo Venier dei Leoni
701 Dorsoduro
30123 Venice
Italy
www.guggenheim-venice.it

Moderna Museet
Box 163 82 Stockholm
SE-103 27 Stockholm
Sweden
www.modernamuseet.se

The Museum of Modern Art
(Under renovation until 2005.
See web site for further details.)
11 West 53 Street
New York, NY 10019
www.moma.org

National Gallery of Art
6th Street and Constitution Avenue, NW
Washington, DC 20565
www.nga.gov

Staatsgalerie
Postfach 10 43 42
70038 Stuttgart
Germany
www.staatsgalerie.de

Tate Modern
Bankside
London SE1 9TG
www.tate.org.uk

Index